Snippets

Of

Life,

Love,

And

Living

By C.A.R.

PublishAmerica
Baltimore

Softcover 978-1-4626-4595-4
PUBLISHED BY PUBLISHAMERICA, LLLP
www.publishamerica.com
Baltimore

Printed in the United States of America

Mom & Dad Rock x

A keepsake of
my work for
you!

Love Cindy

Acknowledgements

This book of verse could not have been possible without the inspiration and creativity given me from my Creator above.

I would like to thank my wonderful family, and friends along the way, who have encouraged me to keep writing, and expressing my feelings through poetry.

A very special tribute needs to be made to my dear friend, and mirror image…

Jerry Stolarski, who took the time to show me that everything worthwhile, all desires in fact, are possible, when they are visualized, and positively accepted as truth already received.

"Time tends to take turns as both friend and foe, and to navigate Life's Path brings joy and woe." {Please enjoy these Snippets of Life, Love, and Living with me. C.A.R.}

Twin Tribute

Though a border may divide us, and at times opinions vary,
Through thick and thin we thus are kin, so life is far less scary;
On land, at sea, and air above, united we stand in peace and love.
Protecting each other sisters, and brothers,
Sharing, discovering, Father Sky, and Earth Mother,
Both our countries are strong and true;
Freedom by democracy sees us through.
Diversity of cultures, language, and faith,
Provides enrichment, empathy, excitement, and grace.
Similar occupations, music, and dance,
So immigrants see unity, and hope at first glance;
May we always be welcoming and hold our heads high,
For we are two great nations with wisdom and pride!

Flying Free

A prayer or two flew way up high on Eagle's wing today;
The angels then retrieved and sent them further on their way;
Prayers going up, and blessings coming down,
Close family ties the whole world round!

Ribbons of Life

The beauty of the sunset, pink with orange and gold,
Decks the skyline majesty with glories new and old;
In the vastness that it fills from clouds to mountain peak,
The whisperings of angels surround you as they speak.
Marshmallow clouds envelope, a staircase cascades down,
Inviting souls to Heaven, their joyful hearts abound;
In this tranquil moment, loved ones never know,
The peaceful celebration that Heaven dost bestow.
One day it will be our turn, to tread that staircase fair,
Encircling ever upward, to meet our family there;
For now we share each moment, until then each eve sunset,
Since we're all found in the tapestry that Heavenly threads connect!

Days of Our Lives

Each day holds either clouds or sun, depending how you are;

Through rain you seem the only one, who seeks the sun afar.

But finally the sun shines through, warming up the sorrow;

Creating happiness anew, and peace for your tomorrow.

The Progressing Journey

A baby's cry is so unique, with hands upheld for love;
They whimper for they cannot speak, and trust in God above.
With little moves they slowly crawl, when leaning soon they stand;
Curiously they walk the hall, reaching for mom's hand.
Using a spoon is something new, as it seems too big to use;
They wonder then what they should do,
and it's fingers they often choose.
The months go by and pages turn, and soon your precious jewel,
Is coming home for noontime meals, then going back to school!

Faith

Faith is something more should hold,
It conquers all life's fears;
It stays within, and can't be sold,
And keeps your heart from tears.

The Best Gift of All

He sat inside the park each day, with breadcrumbs at his side;
He did God's work in his own way, and had nothing to hide.
The friends he knew were only birds, that came so faithfully;
He didn't utter many words, but watched them round his knee.
The birds would sit up in the trees, from dawn till setting sun;
They'd eat, then sing their melodies, but soon the bread was done.
Silently he'd walk away, and was alone once more;
He'd have that bag of crumbs next day, and sit there like before.
This man may seem so very frail, but God cares from above;
His heart could really tell a tale, for what he gave was love!

Music

Music is a special feeling, found deep inside of some;
It has its own natural way of dealing, with sorrow and with fun.
The different kinds of melodies, when sung show how we feel;
Your inner thoughts form harmonies, and thus your tune is real.

Laughter

Laughter is a small emotion, yet you feel so good;
Take time out from life's commotion,
Laugh a bit, you should!

Canyon Gift of Love

The steady hum along the track, with intermittent clickety-clack,
Subsides only for childhood squeals,
and one last call for breakfast meals.
Life whirls by quick as can be, buildings, and train yards,
dot the scenery;
Families wave with a cheery hello, from backyards,
and greenhouses far below.
Further in the distance yet, mountains meet sky unless we forget;
A Mightier Hand carved the beauty around...
we scarcely encompass it from the ground.
From high within the coach we see,
the splendor meant for you and me;
Trees abreast the mountain peak, whisper for they cannot speak.
The Lord stretches His Hand across the land,
pleading with us to obey His command;
"Take care of each other, live well, and then,
enjoy My Gifts beloved friends!"

Love

Love is like a blooming rose;
As days go by the feeling grows.
From your heart you do express,
Your thoughts and dreams for happiness.

This House We Call Home

A house has just the walls and floors, with coverings overhead;
There's furniture and closing doors, so why have people said,
That this to them is home sweet home? It seems so vaguely wild.
But this to them is also known, it holds parents and child.
So when you think of your ole place, the little bird above,
Will tell you that to fill this space, you have to have the love!

A Quiet Cry

I only wish I had great faith, the kind that Christ speaks of;
I only wish I had great faith, abounding with my love.
I try so very desperately, to pray and show my care;
A little more faith would be so grand, in answer to my prayer.
I know I'm far from perfect, but I'd like to be like Christ;
I will keep trying every day, in hopes each day is bright.
I only wish I had great faith, the kind that Christ speaks of;
With prayerful asking everyday, I know mercy will come from
above!

What Is A Friend

A friend is someone who is near, trustworthy and very dear;
A friend is someone who is kind,
knows your faults but doesn't mind.
A friend is someone strong, and true, who believes in all you do;
A friend is always by your side, one with whom you can confide.
A friend is special through, and through;
A friend is someone, just like you!

Empathy through Prayer

Should tonight you find yourself awake and cannot rest,
Take time to ponder then offer up prayer, for those not at their best.
Quietly just think upon the hurting ones you know;
Lift their names up to the Lord, telling Him you love them so.
When we think of others' woes and put our own aside,
We often find an inner peace our own issues subside.
Empathy for each other is a caring from the heart;
A kiss, a smile, or blessings wished, is a perfect place to start!

Teachers

A teacher has a special way, of dealing with the kids today.
Techniques to learn and notes to write,
that homework's really out of sight,
Their careful choice of words and praise,
with patience on the slower days,
The extra help when needed true, extensions when an essay's due,
Helpful hints and cooking tips, positioning words with opened lips,
Hints for remembering history dates, forgiving inexcusable lates,
Yes teachers care and really try, to help you pass your
school-years by;
In doing so they help you be, active parts of society.

Five-Sense Wonder

May our eyes see goodness but be blind to others' faults.
May our ears hear only truth, and shun deception.
May our lips taste all the sweetness life has to offer, and refrain from the bitterness.
May our noses detect the scent of kindred spirits, and scuttle from the enemy lurking.
May our hearts absorb echoes of dreams, hopes, and wishes that are truly pure, enabling them to take flight in a proper time and place!

Time Slides By

The hands of time move steady and slow, tick, tock, tick, tock;
The class awaits patiently ready to go, tick, tock, tick, tock.
With pen and paper we hurriedly write, tick, tock, tick, tock;
Quickening scribbles, "oh what a sight" tick, tock, tick, tock.
Take up assignments and put away books, tick, tock, tick, tock;
The end draws near and everyone looks, tick, tock, tick, tock.
The clock on the wall continues its song, tick, tock, tick, tock;
The time has come to move along, tick, tock, tick, tock.

The Enticing Endeavour Dance

At the onset of our journey anticipation rules;
Potential friends await us, learning sparks on entering school.
The learning floor beckons to us, embracing joys and woes;
Passionate partners lead us through, fleeting knowledge they bestow.
At times we saunter, flit, or glide; we vacillate until,
The rhythm of our true success, displays confidence and skill.
All too soon the music's ending, and persistence brought us through,
Trusting, hoping, dreaming, thanks for this learning dance with you!
Thank you Teachers!

Born to Fly

Long ago you were so tiny, and dependant on all;
You followed by examples, afraid that you might fall.
You flit from task to talent, crawled first, now you climb;
You showed advancement ever upwards,
new knowledge to combine.
The safety nets surround us, kind gestures, words, and faces,
Doubtful of the miles ahead, yet too soon you finished races.
Teaching partners led the way, with hope and happy cheers;
They watched with pride dear little one,
at times their eyes held tears.
So as you stand before us, graduates now to be,
A chapter of your life's complete, but the finale's yet to see.
As you spread your wings now, the future's yours to plot;
Please look back with well-earned pride, keep learning,
and never stop.
Although we sure will miss you, your limit's now the sky;
You are each one a treasure, so keep gliding butterfly!

The Blanket of Surprises

Before you is the darkened path of opportunities;
Its story now is incomplete, so create it as you please.
Before you is the darkened path of challenges so great;
Meeting them is up to you so please don't hesitate.
Before you is the darkened path of moments bright and blue;
Find the best in everything, for then hassles are few.
Before you is the darkened path, but behind you it is light;
Ahead of you you'll notice soon, a rainbow is in sight!

Rising Stars

A drop of love became a bubble, days of praise,
or sometimes trouble;
Playing dolls or banging drums, racing cars, just having fun,
Carefree days soon filled with school, and setting life's course
became the rule.
Tying shoes, learning to spell, favourite colours,
what would you tell?
A tiny boy became a man and a little girl, a young woman.
The latest song or trendy clothes, lessons were learned from what
they chose;
Taking notes, cramming for tests, procrastination, and all the rest,
Insistent teachers, and strong-willed kids, life lessons were learned,
a myriad;
The road you travelled was sometimes rough; At times you fell and
it was tough.
Teaching partners led the way, and urged you on to brighter days;
So as you take your leave from here,
you might look back and shed a tear.
From K to 12 where did time go? Am I ready? I just don't know.
Trepidation, confidence too, joy, and sorrow might all ensue;
You'll stand firm and find your place,
engaging tasks with grit and grace.
So much more to ascertain, yet your mark on Earth shall remain;
Your disposition and talents too, will intertwine with others who,
Rise up and sing a brand new song; giving hope to this World who's
waited so long!
A rainbow of colours, shapes, and sizes, answer the cries as your
wisdom rises;
From love you were formed; A miracle you are, you're each unique
and a shining star!

Emotions

This tree has infinite branches, like sorrow, love, or pain;
Your mind has numerous chances, to feel these like the rain.
Some folks try to disguise these, and let them hide within;
Yet some will show like blooming trees, and thus you just can't win.
Emotions come in many forms, from pouting to a smile;
They come as often as a storm, each only lasts a while.

There Is A Way

Life's uncertainties are great, with many different forms;
Life's uncertainties are great, and mount just like a storm.
Life's uncertainties are great, with problems everywhere;
Life's uncertainties are great, corrupted folks aren't rare.
Life's uncertainties are great, and blossom every day;
Life's uncertainties are great; it's hard to find your way.
Life's uncertainties are true, so deciphering them is up to you!

Mercy Please Oh Mercy

Can a broken heart be ever put together? Can one's shattered dreams
be ever reconciled?
Can mistakes be ever turned around? Can a child through desperate
cries be found?
Can a future goal ever be attained? Can a hard-taught lesson press
firm upon one's heart?
Can a brief acquaintance ever cross your way, bringing future peace
and love to stay?
Can a parent forget a child or will they ever be, strong, and loving,
forgiving too, as merciful as can be? I'll hope with all my heart and
soul, and ne're forget to pray;
Through good and bad, happy, or sad, God shall abide with me each
day!

Darkness of Light

My life was once so lonely, and my world was once so small;
My thoughts were once so dismal, that I felt three inches tall.
The walls seemed to surround me, and the joys I held were few;
The friends I had were helpful, but knew not what to do.
I couldn't understand it, and I didn't want to try;
I had continual nightmares, and once, watched myself die.
One day my life turned pleasant, and it seemed my world was bright;
That day my thoughts were happy, and a rainbow was in sight.
Those walls seemed to recede now, and the joys I held increased;
My friends were still so helpful, and troubles then had ceased.
Now I understood it, and I knew just what to do;
Now my dreams are pleasant, and it's all because of you!

Strength Whispers in the Breeze

As the storm subsides and gentle rains scatter, I must decide what's
truly the matter;
The sun tries to shine a scarce little bit, but is at last lost through the
cloud's angry fit.
The rainbow is mocked and pushed far aside, but yet in my heart I
must always abide;
Despite the abuse, guilt, and shame, the sun tries to fight through the
wind and the rain.
At last then fair-weather through this torment and fear, I will
somehow grasp gentle breezes and steer. I'll fly through the storms,
the thunder, and lightning;
Along with sweet breezes, life's far less so frightening!

33

That Sparkle in Your Eyes

It happened oh so suddenly while walking slowly home;
It happened oh so suddenly, I felt a bit alone.
It happened oh so suddenly, when speaking face to face;
It happened oh so suddenly, when shyly we embraced.
It happened oh so suddenly, when whispering "I love you;"
It happened oh so suddenly and finally I knew.
Our love will last a lifetime through, for now I know our love is
true!

Playing the Odds

Love is just a simple word, with only letters four;
Yet love is a very complex word, ambiguous and bold.
Love can be so very kind, or love can be quite cruel;
Yes love has many meanings, and they aren't all taught in school.
Love can be a moonlit kiss, or love can be an angry cry;
Love can be a promise grand, or love can be a kiss good bye.
Love can be a special night, or love can be a caring thought;
Love can be a one night stand, or love can really mean a lot.
Love can be so cutting, but love can also be quite true;
You simply have to take a chance, in hopes the effort sparks a dreamy hue!

A Special Someone

I know a special someone, who really understands;
I know a special someone, who cares but ne're demands.
I know a special someone, who showed me how to give;
I know a special someone, who makes me want to live.
I know a special someone, who is so very true;
I know a special someone, who believes in all I do.
I know a special someone, faithful through and through;
I know this special someone, just happens to be you!

A Ray of Sunshine

Your eyes they always sparkle;
Your hands are always warm.
Your smile's always cheery,
And clears away the storm.
Whenever I am worried,
Whenever I feel blue,
Whenever I'm unhappy,
You know just what to do.

Abide With Him Lord

Nobody else may ask You this, but yet I feel I should;
Please be with him Father, through bad times and the good.
He didn't mean to hurt me, or change my way of life;
Please be with him Father, in this time of strife.
Help him learn to live his life, in an adult sort of way;
Please be with him Father, to be stronger day by day.
May he learn to be like Christ, strong, and true, and kind;
Please be with him Father, and help him use his precious mind.

Nature

Nature is of many things

Just for one a bird that sings

Grasses green and growing strong

Sun and rain to help along

Snowfalls and a chilling breeze

Maples and their falling leaves

Cold blue waters flowing by

Above your head the sweeping sky

Creatures darting to and fro

Sand you're walking on below

Yes... Nature is a pretty scene

Let's all together keep it clean!

Words of Wisdom

We saw a Bald Eagle today;
Two Falcons swooped by him at play.
Mallards discussed the rattling fuss,
as the Zephyr beside them did sway.
"What is that strange beast, with diesel to feast?
The fumes it creates, our habitat devastates!"
Said the fleet Dapple Grey, "It holds folks I daresay!"
"Mountain Goat do you know, where does that beast go?"
"That beast it doth brings, travelers to…The Springs!
They rest and refresh until feeling their best!"
"It just seems to me, yaps the noisy Osprey…
Humans' lives are a mess! They seek counsel I guess,
from we smart-living birds and beasts!"

Heart Sense

If heart could see...what would it be?
A thousand missed opportunities?
If heart could hear...what echoes cry?
Hawks and Eagles in the sky?
If heart could smell...what stories tell?
The cognizant scent where nature dwells?
If heart could taste...what essence then?
A delicious kiss that never ends?
If heart could touch...what would it do?
Embrace and bring love close to you!

Springtime Blues

Blue sky up high, ocean down low,
Eagles fly and Orcas blow.
Mating doves above you coo;
Grass is damp with morning dew.
Deer prance by admiring the view.
Seagulls dip without a clue;
To grab a crab or maybe two.
In the distance something's new;
A tiny calf blurts out a "Moo…"
She's saying spring is here, rainbows too;
Love is in the air, so don't be blue!

Spring

As the last flakes of snow melt deep in the Earth,

The world's ready now for upcoming spring birth.

As many new birds come back from afar,

My mind wanders back to my dream-filled star.

I dream on of kids swinging, and new birds when singing,

Blue skies and a breeze, whistling through the trees,

Schools of fish in the brooks, but when one quickly looks,

Our spring is now done, giving way to summer sun.

Summertime

Summertime brings those fun-filled days, of swimming,
and gardening too,
The warmth of blessed summer rays and many things to do;
There's weeding plants and trimming trees,
and don't forget the lawn,
Mother stops to catch a breeze, but soon she's urged along.
The roses bloom and children play, while others sweep the walk;
Families plan their holiday, with suitcases to lock.
Yes summer means so many things, unique for everyone;
Fall's what Old Man Season brings, with school, then summer's
done!

Waves upon the Ocean

It beckons me to come near,
Each new time I pass by here;
It draws me into her misty blue,
Crying for me as I cry for you!

Soaring Love

As I drove along today, the ocean swells looked dark and grey;
Beckoning for me to hear, their tale of woe and message clear.
"A friend or two they need your prayers, so please take time to show you care!"
So as I take this word to heart, a gift of love I shall impart;
I send my hugs and kisses too, in hopes you feel my love flow through.
Angels and Eagles fly it there; Hope is coming on a wing and a prayer!

The Sonnet of the Tap-Root Kings

Tap-root seedlings they began,
Stomped down in post-fire soil;
Slurping nutrients from high-quartz sand,
Yet drought would scarcely spoil.
Forty, maybe eighty years,
Between clear-cut rotations,
The least productive of its peers,
Yet pride of logging nations.
They didn't like it boggy,
And they shied from alkaline;
They tolerated sometimes soggy,
But dry earth would usually win.
Sparse-crowned kings of Mother Earth,
Use them wisely; Allow rebirth!

Wisdom of the Woods

Skirted outline majesty, bedecked of green and gold,
Wistfully a chanting, of mysteries young and old;
Grandeur oh most glorious, sway softly to and fro,
Dreamily dance and beckon, spirited ones to grow!

The Fury of Winter

Through storms and gusty billows you prevail;
Your icy finger points towards the Earth.
Cold temperatures hold fast just as a nail;
On roads ice clings just like a horse's girth.
Our cars are buried deep beneath the snow;
Vauntingly you laugh at what you've done.
As dawn breaks through transmissions cease to go;
Once again you've had your jot of fun.
Seasons come and go just like a tide;
Winter you'll elapse just as before.
To "Old Man Season's" rules you must abide,
And give your puissant reign to "Spring" once more.
Alas… "Old Winter Friend," proceed to bring,
Your crafty tricks whilst I await the "Spring!"

St. Nicholas

St. Nicholas can you hear me for this is but my wish,
That every hungry child could have food upon their dish;
No more wars, or hatred, no diseases, pain, or fear,
That every word one utters, and every gesture be sincere.

Christmas

Christmas is a special time when loved ones gather near,
To welcome in the New Year with tidings of good cheer.
Christmas means much more than fun to many as you know.
It reminds us of Christ Jesus, Who was born so long ago.
We remember how the angels sang of peace to men on Earth,
And Wisemen with their gifts most rare, offered at His birth.
The shepherds fearful as they saw the angel that did say,
What special happening did occur and where the Babe did lay.
We must not leave out Joseph, Earthly Father of This Child,
And His Mother Mary, so loving, meek, and mild.
What about the birds and beasts that round about did stay,
To watch the new Babe Jesus, Who in the manger lay?
You see Christmas really does mean more than Santa high above;
It reminds us of a "Shining Star", and Our Redeemer's Love!

Sharing the Spotlight

Blue skies up above, sunshine and ocean breeze,
Says hello Spring/Summer, and good bye Winter freeze.
You had your jot of fun, so I'll show you to the door;
We shall welcome you back, when it's your turn once more.

I Wonder

The wind is blowing softly;
The sun is shining through.
The trees are gently waving;
The sky is ever blue.
The world seems to be peaceful,
Yet my heart is full of pain;
Will my soul be ever carefree,
Or will it tumble like the rain?

The Winter of Her Life

The once tiny shoot burst from fertile ground,
Growing and blossoming with love that she found.
Stronger, more vibrant with beauty so rare,
And on one passing glance it would seem without care.
Through sunlight and shadows, fair-winds and storm,
The once stunning beauty began to change form.
Her colour was fading, and life-blood was weak;
The world kept on humming and didn't hear her speak.
One grey morning her presence was gone;
She wilted and gave up her struggle before dawn.
Passers-by left to merely ask why,
She was such a dear treasure so how could she die?
But wait, there's a lesson within all this sorrow;
Celebrate ALL life around us, for brighter tomorrows!

Just a Whisper on the Wind

Nobody should ever feel alone, alone enough to cry;
Nor ever feel insignificant, enough to want to die.
We all should cherish everyday, as if it were our last;
Lift brothers and sisters along the way, giving hope and happiness.
Share a seed of friendship with a smile, a tender hug, or kiss;
Take a moment just to chat a while, tell a hurting soul they're missed.
Visit the sick and lend a hand, When' ere you get the chance;
Find the silver lining in every cloud; let's help this sad ole world to
dance!

Just For Today

Just for today…
May our arms reach further…
Our legs pump harder…
Our eyes see more clearly random acts of kindness, and senseless
sights of beauty…
Our ears hear more intricately the sounds of nature…
Our lips taste the milk of human kindness…
Our nostrils breathe in deeply the calming scents and spice of life…
And our minds embrace the balance of hope, and peace that is just
around the corner!
Just for today take a moment to…
Remember how you are ever intertwined in a "Mighty Circle of
Life" with loving brothers and sisters everywhere!

The Subtle Clutch

Death for me seems close at hand; perhaps my time has come at last.
It's time to think of long ago, of happy times and sad as well.
I think of laughing, joking, pleading, crying,
new and cherished love affairs,
Broken hearts and many tears.
Shall I prod along in hopes of happiness?
This may end once again in loneliness.
Perhaps it is best to open that little bottle and toss back the capsules
of quickening time, to end the pain forever;
I shant, no I can't, and allow those tearful faces to mourn my passing.
I must try to trust in the awakening sun, and God's gentle touch;
From now until then, I must put forth a smile e'en though my heart
holds the scars of many memories.

Let's Count Our Blessings

We are so very fortunate to have our senses five;
And in our joy we do forget those struggling to survive.
Our friends and neighbours without sight whose daily lives are grey,
They cannot see the sunset bright nor watch the children play.
There are others who can't hear the sound of voices loud and clear;
They rely upon the ears around to tell them what they hear.
There are some who cannot speak in words like others can;
They just communicate each day with motions of their hands.
There are those who cannot move their hands to hold a cup of tea;
They struggle just so they may stand, and shall never climb a tree.
Still others cannot smell a thing not even food they eat,
Nor flowers when they bloom in spring, so life is incomplete;
When we touch, smell, hear, or sing, and see how others are,
Let's count our every blessing, for we're luckier by far!

A Bouquet of Forget-Me-Nots for My Savior

I heard a knocking at the door and thrust it open wide;
Standing there before me was a sight that made me cry.
Jesus held His Arms out pleading... "Might I come inside?"
"Yes!" seemed appropriate to say, yet I shook with fear;
Why had the Savior come to me...a mom so plain and drear?
With sadness showing in His Eyes, He softly spoke to me;
"We need to have a heart to heart, there's pain that shouldn't be!"
With that He whisked me through the door,
but what was this I found?
Not sky, not sun, not bird of air, no living soul around.
As if in dream I fell asleep and saw a hall of doors;
Dear Jesus said, "Now pick one for we have a lot of chores!"
The minutes passed, and one by one we visited each room;
We dusted out bad memories of anger, fear, and gloom.
At last he said, "We're finished...the wrongs are put to right!"
"Dear Little one, I'll leave you now, your heart is pure and light!"
"My Spirit's here to guide you, pray often, come to Me!"
"For when you feel the most alone, beside you I shall be!"

New Route

I prayed the unbeliever's prayer this morning,
and on my knees I spent,
A quiet time just God and I, and to Heaven those prayers went.
I cried out for help you see, to take the pain away,
Replacing it with courage, to face another day.
Yesterday was awful as I tried to reach once more,
The closed-heart of a "could- be- friend," who once was,
but is no more.
While asking for this one's closed heart to soften just a bit,
I also asked my Father to work in me and never quit.
Please take away all anger, insecurities, fear, and doubt.
Dust, and sweep, and buff me up till I can smile and shout...
My Creator is so awesome! Non-stop to the top...
"New Route!"

Hummingbird Me

Teach me to hum your tender tune;
To vacillate swiftly, content to sojourn.
Squelch my inhibitions and illuminate my lot;
I'm presently inconsequential, but one day yearned and sought.

The Potter's Perfection

Refuse to be stomped on as yesterday's fire;
We're healthy, and worthy, with future desires.
God doesn't make junk though unpolished we be;
One day a fine vessel is what you'll all see!

A Glimpse Beyond

We curve along the canyon pass, through tunnels many but alas,
There is no fear from deep within,
as soon we're called to the light again.
Darkness of Earth, frailty of life,
surges us forward amidst daily strife;
A brief glimpse of struggle, through death we must pass,
To the glory of Heaven, our destination at last!

Love-light In the Night Sky

I should like to be a star, twinkling high above;
Peeking through Heaven's Floor to those below I love.
Holding each one's hopes and fears, delivering each one,
So Our Creator blesses them from dawn till setting sun.

Dreams Are…

Dreams are the wishes calling from our hearts to be fulfilled.
Dreams keep our minds fresh, young, hope-filled, and connected
to Heaven above;
Angels and Eagles carry our thoughts to and fro, forward and
back, as life's pendulum sways on!

Dreamy Peace-filled Slumber With Blue/Grey

Darting to and fro, hither and yon Friend Wolf,
You blend in with the sparse, snow-crusted, barren trees;
I find you keeping pace with my fleeting thoughts.
Whether in my dreams, or in my heart,
The Dream catcher truly imparts,
A quest for love, and tender days,
As Wolf stays near to guide my way!

Would you like to see your manuscript become a book?

If you are interested in becoming a PublishAmerica author, please submit your manuscript for possible publication to us at:

acquisitions@publishamerica.com

You may also mail in your manuscript to:

PublishAmerica
PO Box 151
Frederick, MD 21705

www.publishamerica.com